Discerning God's Call

Discerning God's Call

Helping People Discern God's Call To
Directing the Spiritual Exercises
of St. Ignatius Loyola, 19th Annotation

Ellen Tomaszewski

With the SEEL Tri-Cities Group

Discerning God's Call

Copyright © 2015, 2016, 2017, 2018
Ellen Tomaszewski
ISBN: 978-1-936824-57-1

&
etcetera press

Etcetera Press LLC; Richland, WA 99352

The material in this manual is copyrighted. Please purchase a registered copy for your use and those in your group.

Contents

Discernment Year Introduction 7
Chapter 1 19
Examen 30
Chapter 2 31
Chapter 3 43
Chapter 4 50
Chapter 5 56
Chapter 6 62
Chapter 7 68
Chapter 8 78
Chapter 9 80
Appendix A 82
Appendix B - Guidelines for Ethical Conduct 93
Purpose and History 100

Discernment Year Introduction

Why a Discernment Year

The Spiritual Exercises of St. Ignatius of Loyola (19th Annotation) program is often run by lay people, for lay people. When those who participate as directors are often not trained in spiritual direction, (such as a seminary or place of higher learning) they are often trained by other directors.

To ensure that the program continues, and that new people are able to participate as directors, our group, the Spiritual Exercises in Everyday Life Tri-Cities, had to find a way to train people to become Spiritual directors.

We realized that most people weren't ready to jump from praying through the Exercises to directing them. So this year of discernment was formed.

Those called to direction have a process to discern God's call. During this year, people have the opportunity to pray, discuss, and consider the commitment and the skills needed to do a good job directing the Spiritual Exercises in Everyday Life, and whether they have the desire and time to pursue such a call.

Just as Jesus spent time growing and learning for thirty years before his ministry, so too, directors can take time to learn and grow before they begin the directing work during the discernment year. Following this book, each person in the program will have the opportunity to:

- Explore his or her potential
- Discuss with others gifts and their challenges
- Identify places in need of grow or change

Skills that will be focused on include:
- Ministerial gifts
- Mutual as well as individual discernment
- Sharing faith life
- Gifts of a spiritual director

In this protected setting, a person can test and discover his or her calling for the ministry of spiritual direction.

Group Discernment

It's true that each individual is called to consider his or her own vocational direction. However, in spiritual direction, there is an added communal aspect. It is in the spirit of discernment – a call within the community and with the community – that we present this program.

Discernment Process

This process includes preparation for, and attendance at, eight two-hour meetings and a final one-on-one meeting between discerner and program director or experienced spiritual director. Activities include:
-
- Opening prayer
- Content
- Book discussion
- Individual shares
- Group members respond
- Triad direction practice (if possible)
- Discuss Annotations from the Spiritual Exercises
- Evaluate the meeting
- Prepare for the next meeting
- Closing prayer

Discernment Facilitator

The person who facilitates the process will be:
- Knowledgeable about discernment
- Already practicing discernment
- Proven to have incorporated many qualities of a spiritual director into his or her life
- Able to understand the dynamics of projection and counter transference
- Willing to risk and challenge, as well as love
- Able to develop an atmosphere of discernment

Time Commitment

In addition to attending discernment meetings, we ask that participants:

- Attend various retreat experiences including the monthly meetings with new retreatants.
- Find a spiritual director and meet with him or her at least once a month. (If you don't have access to one, please let us know and we'll help you with this.)
- Read the books assigned and be prepared to discuss them at the meetings.

Meeting Summary

Meetings will last about two hours. Each meeting has an agenda can be found in this book.

Qualities of a Spiritual Director

According to the Institute for Theological Studies at Seattle University, and Spiritual Directors International, these are some aspects of a spiritual director:

Called by God to the work

- Feels or senses that God is calling
- The inner call is confirmed by outer signs, such as being sought out by others

Gifted in interpersonal skills

- Is trustworthy, psychologically mature and in the process of maturing more
- Able to see what God is doing in another
- Is growing in skills of being with another
- Is willing and able to be affected
- Changed by the spiritual direction relationship

Gifted in grace; is a person of faith

- Able to notice the movement of God in another
- Vulnerable and open to the mystery of life
- Developing knowledge of theology, scripture, and spiritual tradition
- Willing to accompany another even though issues might be mysterious and/or challenging

Discernment Year Overview

Meeting 1

- Review the year and its purpose
- Set dates for meetings, confirm participation
- Get assignment for the coming month
- Annotations 1, 2, 3, 5
- Begin reading assigned books

Meeting 2

- Discuss consolation and desolation
- Discuss Chapters 1-4 of *Inviting the Mystic, Supporting the Prophet*
- Share my gifts and call to ministry of Spiritual Direction
- Annotations 11, 12, 13
- Ignatian Discernment Rules # 313 – 336

Meeting 3

- Discuss the second half of Inviting the Mystic, Supporting the Prophet (Chapters 5-9)
- Observe direction session (presented by directors)
- Share how I am clarifying my call - indications
- Annotations 19, 20, Examen (24, 32-43)

Meeting 4

- Listen to presentation: mirror, clarify, & challenge
- Share how I am clarifying my call concerning directing
- Discuss first 4 chapters of Finding God in All Things by William A. Barry, SJ
- Observe direction session and comment
- Annotations 4, 6, 7, 8, 9.

Meeting 5

- Observe direction. Comment with focus on mirroring clarifying, challenging, consolation and desolation
- Share how I'm clarifying my call about directing
- Discuss chapters 5-8, Finding God in All Things
- Annotations 14, 15, 16

Meeting 6

- Share strengths and places I need to grow
- Discuss chapters 9-11, Finding God in All Things
- Practice mirroring, clarifying, and challenging
- Annotations 17, 18, 22
- Observe direction session and comment

Meeting 7

- Discuss the Practice of Spiritual Direction
- Discuss first 60 pages The Art of Christian Listening
- Observe direction session and comment
- Share issues and problems in becoming a spiritual director
- Annotation 170 - 189
- Get instructions for final paper

Meeting 8

- Bring your written feedback to others' papers.
- Finish discussion of The Art of Christian Listening
- Share self-recommendation and feedback to others
- Ignatian Exercises: Annotation 23

Meeting 9 - Follow-up

Meet with the facilitator individually for a final clarification and decision on the nest steps.

Resources

We will use various resources, including:

Required reading:

Please purchase the following books and materials [or those prescribed by the organizers of your program]:
- *Inviting the Mystic, Supporting the Prophet* by L. Patrick Carroll and Katherine Dyckman.
- *The Practice of Spiritual Direction* – Connolly & Barry
- *The Art of Christian Listening* - Thomas Hart
- *Finding God in All Things* by William A. Barry, SJ
- *The Spiritual Exercises of St. Ignatius (*various translations available)
- *Spiritual Directors International Standards for Spiritual Directors* © *2000.* [Copies of these standards can be obtained at the Spiritual Directors International Website, http://*www.sdiworld.org.*]

Other good resources (not required)

- *Women at the Well* – Kathleen Fischer
- *Care of Mind, Care of Spirit* – Gerald May
- *Addiction and Grace* – Gerald May
- *Spirituality and Personal Maturity* – Joann Wolski Conn
- *The Code of Ethics for Spiritual Directors* – Thomas M. Hedber, SDB and Betsy Caprio
- *Spiritual Freedom* – John English S.J.
- *What is Ignatian Spirituality?* – David Flemming, S.J.

Learning Contract

At the first meeting, you will be asked to fill out and sign a learning contract. This helps you know what is expected, and helps solidify your intent.

- Your learning contract can help you remember that this process needs your conscious participation.
- You can choose someone to assist you as your support person of choice, and you can list this person on the form.

Once you fill out the contract, give a copy to your group director. It will be returned to you at the end of the year, before you write your discernment decision paper, so that you can recognize your progress toward program completion.

Meeting Agendas

Chapter 1

Opening Prayer [5 min] - Soul of Christ by David L. Fleming, SJ (A contemporary paraphrase of Anima Christi, a favorite prayer of Ignatius.)

Jesus, may all that is you flow into me. May your body and blood by my food and drink.

May your passion and death be my strength and life. Jesus, with you by my side enough has been given.

May the shelter I seek be the shadow of your cross. Let me not run from the love which you offer. But hold me safe from the forces of evil.

On each of my dyings, shed your light and your love. Keep calling to me until that day comes, when, with your saints, I may praise you forever. Amen.

Welcome and Introductions [45 min]

- Each person introduces self with answer to this question:
    - How are you feeling about the Spiritual Exercises and your relationship to them? (Be honest.)

Presentation [20 min]

- Overview of the Discernment Year process
- Why a discernment year
- Tools used for this discernment
- Qualities of a spiritual director
- Questions and clarification

Break [10 min]

Spiritual Exercises of St. Ignatius Discussion [25 min]

- Review and discuss Annotation 1, 2, 3, 4, 5.

Finalize your decision to participate [10 min]

- Take quiet [3 minutes].
- Read and reread the prayer.
- Fill out contract.

Summary [10 min]

- Set dates for future meetings
- Discuss homework for next meeting
- Review requirements:
    - Receive monthly spiritual direction.
    - Continue your own discernment.
    - Read and come prepared to discuss homework.
    - Pray daily, especially the Examen.
    - You're invited to attend any 19th Annotation Spiritual Exercises group meeting.

Closing Prayer [5 min]

First Principle and Foundation with Suscipe.

Homework

- Please pray with Psalm 139 (page 27) about and journal on the following question and be prepared at our next meeting to discuss your answers.

Question

- As I reflect on my life, what were the key moments in my faith journey that might indicate to me that God is calling me to the ministry of spiritual direction?

Read

- Chapters 1-4 Inviting the Mystic, Supporting the Prophet and come prepared to discuss.
- Read Annotations 11, 12, 13 in the Spiritual Exercises of St. Ignatius. Come prepared to discuss them at the next meeting.
- Pray the Examen every day.
- Arrange to meet with your spiritual director at least once this month.
- Keep a journal of your discernment journey

Discernment Learning Contract

Identify in my own words the main issue that I desire to discern through this discernment year.

Identify one desire that I have, to support my discernment year.
(For example, find a director, become accountable for a daily habit of prayer, seek out wisdom from persons who have been in the ministry of spiritual direction, choose a good book to read on the Exercises, etc.)

What steps can I take to bring my desire into reality? Be specific. How, when, where, what is going to help me achieve this desire?

Do I feel confirmed in my desire when I bring it before God in prayer? Are the steps I listed above confirmed in prayer?

What do I feel called to do this year to support my discernment, now that I've taken time to identify my inner desires, let them become concrete, and brought them to God?

Reward/celebrate:

List some ways I can celebrate my progress along the way to achieve my desire.

Signature _____

Date _____

Support Person's Signature (if desired):

_____

Qualities of a Spiritual Director

These are some elements of a discerning heart and therefore the basis for spiritual direction.

General qualifications

- Enthusiastic for the Exercises of St. Ignatius
- Dedicated to his or her own spiritual journey
- Faithful to prayer
- Often sought out by others for spiritual advice
- Trustworthy
- Preserves confidentiality
- Compassionate - able to accompany another in suffering or joy
- Working toward a mature spirituality

Personal development

- Emotional maturity - can keep retreatant's issues separate from personal issues.
- Can work through conflict effectively.
- Able to give and receive both positive and constructive feedback.
- Knows when to ask for help and does so.

Spiritual development

- Works to develop knowledge and ability to live Ignatian Spirituality.
- Nurtures own spiritual life – prayer & direction.
- Has experience with prayer that uses content and imagery (kataphatic vs. apophatic) and is able to lead others into Ignatian prayer.
- Has made a directed retreat, preferably the 19th annotation.

Social awareness

- Aware of the need for social justice
- Recognizes God in the poor

Community living development

- Comfortable with sharing his or her faith.
- Comfortable leading group prayer, or is open to learning.
- Believes in our mission and is able to commit time to it.
- Committed to participating in community, including in-service training, director meetings, participant meetings, retreats, workshops, etc.

Basic skills required before directing

- Practice and acquire spiritual direction skills.
- Practice and acquire active listening skills.
- Basic knowledge and understanding of the Ignatian "points" of the Spiritual Exercises.

Closing Prayer

The First Principle and Foundation of St. Ignatius

The Goal of our life is to live with God forever. God, who loves us, gave us life. Our own response of love allows God's life to flow into us without limit. All the things in this world are gifts from God, presented to us so that we can know God more easily and make a return of love more readily. As a result, we appreciate and use all these gifts of God insofar as they help us to develop as loving persons. But if any of these gifts become the center of our lives, they displace God.

Thus, they hinder our growth toward our goal.

In everyday life, then, we must hold ourselves in balance before all of these created gifts insofar as we have a choice and are not bound by some obligation. We should not fix our desires on health or sickness, wealth or poverty, success or failure, a long life or a short one.

For everything has the potential of calling forth in us a deeper response to our life in God. Our only desire and our one choice should be this: I want and I choose what better leads to God's deepening his life in me.

With this in mind, we pray Ignatius' prayer:

Suscipe

Take, Lord, and receive all my liberty, my memory, my understanding, and my entire will, all I have and call my own.

You have given all to me. To you, Lord, I return it.

Everything is yours; do with it what you will. Give me only your love and your grace. That is enough for me.

Amen

Preparation Sheet for Discernment Meeting 2

Psalm 139

Oh, Lord, you have probed me and you know me;
You know when I sit and when I stand;
You understand my thoughts from afar.

My journeys and my rest you scrutinize,
With all my ways you are familiar.
Even before a word is on my tongue, behold, O Lord,
You know the whole of it.

Behind me and before, you hem me in and rest your hand upon me. Such knowledge is too wonderful for me, too lofty for me to attain.

Where can I go from your spirit from your presence where can I flee? If I go up to the heavens, you are there.

If I sink to the nether world, you are present there. If I take the wings of dawn, if I settle at the farthest limits of the sea, even there your hand shall guide me, and your right hand hold me fast.

If I say, "Surely the darkness shall hide me, and night shall be my light." For you darkness itself is not dark, and night shines as the day.

Truly you have formed my inmost being;
You knit me in my mother's womb.

I give thanks that I am fearfully, wonderfully made;
Wonderful are your works.

My soul also you knew full well; nor was my frame unknown to you.

When I was made in secret,
I was fashioned in the depths of the earth.

Your eyes have seen my actions;
In your book they are all written;
My days were limited before one of them existed.

How weighty are your designs, O God.
How vast the sum of them!
Were I to recount them, they would outnumber the sands;
Did I reach the end of them, I should still be with you.

Probe me, O God, and know my heart;
Try me and know my thoughts;
See if my way is crooked,
And lead me in the way of old.

Amen.

Examen

(Please practice daily for the next nine months.)

Review

I review the past hour, day, week, month, or year, believing that God is present.

Thanks

I recall gifts God has given me: life, nourishment, shelter, love, friends, etc. and give thanks for them.

Feeling

I notice my thoughts, words, and deeds and especially my emotions. I ask God to help me understand what they tell me about myself.

Focus

I ask God to show me which of my attitudes cause me to grow further from God. I pray for reconciliation and sorrow for sin.

Future

I Praise God for times I've responded with love. I ask for the grace to discern God's will tomorrow and the courage to follow it. Amen.

Chapter 2

Opening Prayer [2 min]

Psalm 139 *(Page 27)*

Welcome and introductions – [10 min]

- How are you feeling about being here?

Assign small groups [1 min]

Presentation on Discernment [10 min]

- Review and discuss Ignatian Discernment Rules # 313 – 336.
- Review rules and handouts.

Group Sharing Introduction [5 min]

Please remember that this is sharing, not problem solving or fact-finding. Others in the group listen while each discerner shares in turn. After the sharing and a time of quiet, it is OK to:
- Clarify- Ask questions to learn specifically what a person is feeling or thinking. Say something like, "Tell me more about …."
- Mirror by focusing on the feelings. "I hear sadness in your voice."
- Affirm – Boil down what a person has said, noticing their emotion. "Sounds like that experience was very powerful and uplifting for you."
- We will discuss these techniques more at our next meeting.

Sharing

As I reflect on my life, what have been the key moments in my faith journey that might indicate to me that God is calling me to the ministry of spiritual direction?

Group Sharing [15 min/person]

Sharing Process
1. Silent prayer [1 min].
2. One individual shares [8 min].
3. Silence [1 min].
4. Group members respond using mirroring, clarifying, and affirming [4 min].
5. Individual shares how it was for them [1 min].
6. Begin process again with next person.

Book Discussion [15 min]

- Chapters 1-4 Inviting the Mystic, Supporting the Prophet.

Spiritual Exercises Annotation Discussion [10 min]

- Discuss Annotations 6-13

Closing prayer [2 min]

We ask for the light of the Holy Spirit, that I might be able to see through God's eyes ...

The gifts I have received during this meeting that I can be thankful for. (Pause)

That I might see through God's eyes: where God has been working during this meeting and this day. (Pause)

That I might see where I cooperated with God and where I have cooperated with evil or avoided what was right. (Pause)

Help me to see through God's eyes the forgiveness God offers me, for the times when I have not been attentive and responsive to God's love. (Pause)

Help me to see through God's eyes how God's spirit will be with me as I leave here, and how the Holy Spirit can guide me through tomorrow. (Pause) ~ Amen

---

Evaluate meeting – how was this for you? *[2 min]*

Homework for Next Meeting

At our next meeting, we'll explore further God's call to us.

For homework:

- Note your interior feelings (affectivity) concerning your involvement in SEEL between now and then.
- Reflect and journal on following discernment questions.
- Read the Preparation Sheet that follows.
- Practice the Examen daily.
- Meet with your spiritual director.
- Read *Inviting the Mystic, Supporting the Prophet,* Chapters 5-9.
- Read *Annotations 16, 19, 20, 24, 32,-43* in the Spiritual Exercises of St. Ignatius.

Discernment

Discernment is a disposition - A state of mind in which I am disposed to certain things.

In discernment, I turn my ear toward, I am willing to consider, and I am ready to think about, the following characteristics:

Desire for Inner Freedom

This allows me to touch the deepest part of my inner being. It is here that I can truly want what God wants.

Desire for Inner Openness

With inner openness, I re-discover in God's time how I need to grow in discernment and trust. I am open to other's input on my growth.

Desire for Inner Trust

In trust I hear, as well as recognize, my response to God, no matter what that is (fear, grief, anger, joy, forgiveness, love, prejudice?). I want to accept the fact that in God all of this is possible and acceptable.

I Check with Myself

- How free am I to respond to God?
- Do I truly want what God wants?
- Am I open to receive the truth of my gifts as well as my limitations?
- At what point do I find myself saying to God, "No,

I can't go any further"?
- Where do I resist God?
- Can I offer that resistance to God?
- Am I able to let God love me, even in areas where I'm unfree, places that I am driven by outside forces, places that I am slightly or greatly addicted? (Money, success, power, time, control, knowledge, work, food, sugar, alcohol, sex, attention, etc.?)
- Can I let God be with me in order to help me grow into my fullest self?

Ignatius' Definitions and Rules for Discernment

Translation: Sr. Laurel Ann Becker, S.S.N.D. Edited by author. Note: numbers in [brackets] refer to paragraph numbers in the Spiritual Exercises *by St. Ignatius.*

Definitions

[316] **Spiritual consolation** describes our interior life. Consolation is overflowing with love for God and for others. Sadness due to your sinfulness can be consolation if it helps you realize you are a sinner while feeling God's love.

[317] **Spiritual Desolation** also describes interior life. It includes anything that causes confusion, disquiet, or separation from God. If you feel blah, confused, doubtful, restless, discouraged, or wretched, that's desolation.

What to do in Consolation

[323] In consolation, prepare for desolation. Appreciate the gift.

[324a] Consolation can provide the opportunity for growth and true humility. Acknowledge with gratitude the gifts received, and recognize the full goodness of God's favor.

What to do in Desolation

[314b] In desolation, look at how strong you are because the Lord is on your side.

[318] The evil spirit guides you during times of desolation. Therefore, when in desolation, stick to the

decision made in consolation. Never change a decision in desolation that you made in consolation.

[319] Pray more, and add penance.

[320] In desolation you have all the grace you need and more besides. God is with you.

[321] If you are tempted to give in to desolation, be strong and hopeful. Think of the consolation that will come or remember the feelings of consolation you felt. Remember how much the Lord loves you. Keep praying!

[322] There are three reasons for desolation:
a) You deserve it.
b) It's a test - are you going to rely on yourself or put your trust in God?
c) It's THE way to know that you are creature and everything is gift. All is grace from the Lord. In desolation, you learn more deeply that you can't do anything without Him.

Recognizing the Evil Spirit

[325] Sometimes the evil spirit acts like a mischievous child, annoying and disturbing you as long as he can get away with it. Tell him to go back to hell where he belongs, and he will go.

[326] Sometimes the evil spirit acts sneaky. He will make friends with you, and convince you that everything he tempts you to do is OK, as long as it is kept as "our little secret." The best thing for you to do is be open, admit you faults and sins.

[327]. Sometimes the evil spirit attacks your weakest points, to topple your resolve and spirit.

Rules that apply when choosing between good and evil

[314] If you are caught in sin, the evil spirit brings up pleasures and images of sensual delights in order to hold you to those bad habits more tightly. God uses the opposite method, pricking and biting your conscience through the process of reason.

[315] If you are trying to choose good and trying to love the Lord (fighting evil,) the evil spirit will do anything to discourage or confuse you. But God is very gentle. You feel peaceful, cheerful, and simple.

Rules that apply when trying to discern between good and God.

[328] When you are **trying to choose between good and God**, God and his angels tend to give support, encouragement, and sometimes even delight.

[329] The evil spirit generally tries to make you feel dissatisfied, anxious about God's love or your response, or he stings your conscience with thoughts of pride about your attempt to lead a good life (desolation.)

[335] **When trying to choose between good and God**, the good spirit will be very delicate, gentle, or delightful. It can be compared to a drop of water on a

sponge. When the evil spirit tries to interrupt that progress, the movement is violent, disturbing, and confusing. It can be compared to the way a waterfall hits a stone ledge. (Note: the opposite happens if you are **choosing evil over good**. See rule [314].)

[330] If you feel consolation without cause - when you didn't have any special thoughts, achievements, events, prayers, or people to create the consolation - consider it to be from God. God alone brings consolation without any outside stimulus.

[336.] When consolation comes without cause, be very careful to distinguish the actual consolation from its afterglow, which may produce joy and exhilaration for a while. During the afterglow, your own human reasoning and other influences enter into decisions.

[332] For a person striving to lead a good life, **trying to choose between good and God,** the evil spirit ordinarily appears as an angel of light (good). For example, you might be inspired by seemingly holy thoughts or desires. But over time, those inspirations lead to pride, selfishness, or preoccupation.

[331] **When trying to choose between good and God**, and you have consolation with cause (Consolation brought by certain thoughts, achievements, events, or emotions) that consolation can be from the evil or good spirit. The good spirit brings consolation that strengthens and speeds progress to Christ.

The evil spirit, on the other hand, arouses good feelings (coming as the 'angel of light' so that we are tempted to focus our attention on wrong things, pursue selfish motives, or place our own will above that of Christ.

[332] For a person trying to **choose between good and God**, the evil spirit ordinarily appears as an "angel of light" (good). For example, you might be inspired by 'holy' thoughts and desires that lead to pride, selfishness, or preoccupation.

[333] In decisions where you are **trying to choose between good and God**, examine the beginning, middle, and end of a decision. If, in reflecting on your thoughts, feelings, and actions, you find that your eyes remained on the Lord, you can be sure that the good spirit had been moving you.

If you realize that you started off well, but thoughts and actions became self-focused or turned you away from God, you should suspect that the evil spirit has twisted a good beginning to an evil direction, and possibly an evil end.

[334] In a choice where you are **trying to choose between good and God**, and you recognize that you have been duped by the evil spirit (you chose good that leads away from God), review all stages through which you passed. Start from the time the evil (or desolation) became apparent and trace back to the good to find where you went wrong. Choose a new direction and be on guard in the future.

Closing prayer

An examination of conscience for the end of the meeting

Let us ask for the light of the Holy Spirit:

That through the eyes of God I may be able to see...

- The gifts that I have received during this meeting that I can be grateful. (Pause for 30 seconds)
- God has been working during this meeting and today.
- Where I collaborated with God and where he collaborated with evil or avoid what was right. (Pause for 30 seconds)
- Help me to see the forgiveness that God offers me, for the moments in which I have not been attentive and receptive to God's love through God's eyes. (Pause for 30 seconds) Help me to see through the eyes of God how the spirit of God will be with me as I go from here, and how the Holy Spirit I can guide through the morning. (Pause for 30 seconds) Amen.

Chapter 3

Welcome and check-in [5 min]

What would you like to share of your life as we gather?

Prayer [5 min]

- Wisdom 8:17, 18, 21, 9:1; 9:10-11

Presentation [10 min]

- Short talk on mirroring, clarifying, affirming, and how to ask questions in ways that invite a person to go deeper.

Direction session [10 min]

- Two directors model a short direction session.

Direction discussion [15 min]

- Group discusses how the director used mirroring, clarifying, affirming, inviting to go deeper.

Sharing on reflection questions [15 min/person]

1. How am I discerning movement of spirits?
2. How do I make decisions? How do I listen within?
3. As a result of being associated with this retreat is there any clearer indication of my call to this ministry?

Sharing Process

1. Invite all to enter into the process.
2. Ask for silence to get centered and prepared to listen to the Spirit [1 min].
3. Individual shares [8 min].
4. Prayerful silence [1 min].
5. Group members respond to presenter (using mirroring, clarifying, affirming, inviting to go deeper) [5 min].
6. Individual shares how he/she experienced the process [1 min].
7. Return to #2 above for the next person.

Book Discussion [15 min]

- Discuss Inviting the Mystic, Supporting the Prophet – Chap. 5-end.

Spiritual Exercises of St. Ignatius [15 min]

- Discuss Annotations 16, 19, 20, 24, 32-43.

Closing Prayer - 1 Corinthians 12: 5-11 [2 min].

Evaluate the meeting [5 min]

Homework

1. Read first five chapters of *Finding God in All Things* by William A. Barry, S.J.
2. Pray about your gifts using 1 Cor 12: 5-11.
3. Attend monthly meeting with new retreatants.
4. Pray the Examen daily.
5. Visit with your spiritual director at least once.
6. Read Ignatian Exercises Annotation 4, 6, 7, 8, 9

Mirror, Clarify, Affirm, Invite and/or Challenge Depth

Sample Presentation (facilitators will bring their own experience and examples)

Mirror - "So it sounds like you are feeling ..."

Listen carefully to unspoken body language as well as words. Repeat in a new way what you heard the person say, repeat back feelings you heard.

One of my retreatants came to me concerned that she had learned little that week. She had spent the week on the same scripture--the storm, traveling on the boat with Jesus and the apostles. She explained how her checkbook was out of balance, yet her husband spent recklessly, and how angry she was at him - the storm of her life.

"You sound angry and hurt."

"Exactly."

After more discussion about her prayer and the scripture she said, "I guess following Jesus doesn't mean you never have hardships. That's new to me. I'm like an apostle. I got afraid in my own storm, and stopped depending on Jesus. I bottle it up. I numb my courage away with food. Or I just stay in bed and stop everything, and feel helpless. I don't want to do that anymore."

This was a major breakthrough for her.

Clarify - "Let me summarize what I heard you say." OR "So I think you are saying ... Am I hearing you correctly?"

Listen carefully, then condense what the person said. Ask questions to understand more clearly what he or she is feeling or thinking.

I had a retreatant in desolation, who couldn't decide whether to take a particular job offer. She felt called to do it, but also hypocritical and afraid. How could she help others due to problems in her own life?

"Let's start at the beginning," I said. "Can you tell me what qualifications you have, and what the job asked for, and how you understand God's call?"

After she told me her qualifications, I said, "I heard you say you're feeling inadequate and afraid. But from what you said, you do have the skills. You seem to be in desolation – feeling distant from God. Is that how you see it?"

"Yes, desolation. Just hearing that helps me a lot. I know fear isn't from God. This has been very helpful," she said. "Would you pray with me, that the Lord take away my hesitations if they aren't from Him?"

Clarifying her turmoil helped her sort out the decision.

Affirm - "Did you notice what happened there? I am impressed that you were able to...."

Tell the person the positive aspects of the experience they have had, and what you perceive she or he learned by that experience.

Often, people don't know if their insights or experiences are getting them any closer to God, or if these events are figments of their own imaginations. Affirmation help the person sort that out.

One of my retreatants went to the wedding feast of Canaan (in prayer) where she saw a little child outside, not invited. She was very concerned with this child, but felt compelled to go into the wedding feast. Inside, to her relief, she found Jesus also very concerned with this child. Jesus went out and got the little girl. Suddenly, the woman recognized the child as herself. She and the child fused and became one.

Jesus brought her into the feast, (which symbolized life for this woman). Jesus comforted her; he told her she was his guest. She felt again reconnected with life. With Jesus she belonged; she was invited. In prayer, she cried, overwhelmed with emotion.

It had been a very powerful consolation, but by the time she met with me, she discounted her experience. "I must have invented it all," she offered.

I said, "Tell me more." After more discussion, I said, "It seems to me that you were given a gift to feel Jesus direct love for you."

She said, "Really? When I think of it that way, I feel affirmed and loved."

Invite and challenge to go deeper - "It might be a good idea if you.... Have you considered...?" Would you consider going back to that again and praying about ...?

Remain prayerful during direction. Listen carefully to how the directed person might be draw closer to God. Ask the Lord if you should share it.

One of my retreatants had a dream where she was in church, hiding from the priest. Naked and embarrassed about it, she hesitated to share it with me. She thought it to be sexual in some way, and felt ashamed that church and priests should be connected to nakedness.

"Would you like to explore this issue?" I asked.

She was willing, and we talked a bit about it, but came to no clear understanding.

"Perhaps during your prayer time this week, you could take this dream to Jesus," I told her. Think about your uncomfortable feelings. Ask the Lord to help you find out where, in you, they are coming from. She squirmed, but agreed.

With further prayer, the woman learned that she felt too vulnerable in the presence of a certain priest, too spiritually naked. She decided that she wanted to get past that and learn how to grow closer to the Lord through her spiritual vulnerability.

Another time, an older woman was praying about her own death, and felt sadness that she hadn't accomplished anything. It was a deep, fearful sadness. Then she felt guilty for wanting to "accomplish" things.

"After all, shouldn't we want to do just what God wants?" she wondered.

I said, "Tell me about the sadness. What values, needs, losses are you sad about?"

She thought a while. "It's not activities; I want to complete *myself*. The thought that I might die before I'm whole and complete – the way God wants me – that's really sad. How can I break down the walls that keep me from doing God's will?"

If she hadn't been challenged to go deeper, she might not have connected her sorrow to her need to grow closer to God.

Summary

These techniques can be used in every direction session to help your directee move closer to Christ, and deepen understanding of what happened in their prayer session. Use them often.

Chapter 4

Welcome and check-in [5 min]

- What would you like to share of your life as we gather?

Opening Prayer: Prayer of Detachment [5 min]

I beg of you, my Lord, to remove anything which separates me from you and you from me.

Remove anything that makes me unworthy of your sight, your control, your reprehension; of your speech and conversation, of your benevolence and love.

Cast from me every evil, that stands in the way of my seeing you; hearing, tasting, savoring, and touching you; fearing and being mindful of you; knowing, trusting, loving, and possessing you; being conscious of your presence and as far as may be, enjoying you.

This is what I ask for myself and earnestly desire from you. Amen.

~ Blessed Peter Faber S.J.

Presentation [10 min]

- Talk on Guidelines for Ethical Conduct

Questions for Reflection and Discussion [10 min]

- How might these guidelines contribute to your practice of spiritual direction?
- Do any of the guidelines we talked about challenge you? If so, how?

Direction Session [10 min]

- *Two* directors model session.

Sharing on reflection questions [15 min/person]

- What am I discerning about the movement of spirits in me?
- How do I make decisions? How do I listen inside myself?
- As a result of being associated with this retreat is there any clearer indication of my call to this ministry?

Sharing Process:
1. Invite all to enter into the process.
2. Ask for silence to get centered and prepared to listen to the Spirit [1 min].
3. Individual shares [8 min].
4. Prayerful silence [1 min].
5. Group members respond to presenter (using mirroring, clarifying, affirming, inviting to go deeper) [5 min].
6. Individual shares how he/she experienced the process [1 min].

8. Return to step 2 for the next person.

Book Discussion [15 min]

- Discuss first 4 chapters of *Finding God in All Things* by William A. Barry, S.J.

Spiritual Exercises of St. Ignatius Discussion [20 min]

- Read and discuss Ignatian Annotations 4, 6, 7, 8, 9.

Closing Prayer [2 min]

- Repeat "Prayer of Detachment" (Pg. 53).

Evaluate the meeting [5 min]

- How was this meeting for you?

Homework

- Read chapters 4-8 in Finding God in All Things by William A. Barry, SJ
- Continue praying the daily Examen.
- See your director at least once this month.
- Read Annotations 14, 15, 16 in the Spiritual Exercises.
- Pray about your gifts using 1 Cor. 12: 5-11.
- Attend Spiritual Exercise 19th Annotation group meeting (if available).

Prayer of Detachment

By Blessed Peter Faber S.J.

I beg of you, my Lord, to remove anything which separates me from you and you from me.

Remove anything that makes me unworthy of your sight, your control, your reprehension; of your speech and conversation, of your benevolence and love.

Cast from me every evil, that stands in the way of my seeing you; hearing, tasting, savoring, and touching you; fearing and being mindful of you; knowing, trusting, loving, and possessing you; being conscious of your presence and as far as may be, enjoying you.

This is what I ask for myself and earnestly desire from you.

Amen.

Peter Faber S.J. (1506-1546) was one of the original companions of St. Ignatius. Ignatius considered Faber most gifted in directing the Spiritual Exercises. This prayer is from Hearts on Fire – Praying with the Jesuits *[P 25].*

Ethical Conduct Guidelines

From the Jesuit provincials of the United States and English Speaking Canada *(See Appendix for full text)*

Terms:
- Directee – Person who comes for direction.
- Spiritual Direction – Listening and being present to a person, to help him or her discover where God is working in every aspect of life, including prayer, relationships, work, family, and more.
- Consultation – Seeking advice from a more experienced director about an issue encountered during spiritual direction. Consultation focuses on the directee and how to accommodate or address his or her issue.
- Supervision – a structured time where the director discusses his or her responses to a spiritual direction session. Supervision focuses on the director.
- Formation – The process of preparing a person to become a spiritual director.

Personal Spiritual Formation

Those who would give the *Exercises* to others will:

- Have completed the full four "weeks" of the Spiritual Exercises under annotation 19 or 20 (testified to by the director);
- Be in personal spiritual direction for at least two years;
- Make annual retreat or training;
- Have discerned a call to this ministry;
- Be a fully initiated Roman Catholic in good

standing for at least three years or a similarly invested member of another Christian denomination who is respectful of, and comfortable with, Roman Catholicism.

Standards for Spiritual Directors

Please read and discuss Section 1 of Appendix 2.
Spiritual Director and the Self
- Spiritual directors assume the responsibility for personal growth....
- Spiritual directors engage in ongoing formation as directors ....
- Spiritual directors engage in supervision and/or consultation ....
- Spiritual directors meet their needs outside the spiritual direction relationship in a variety of ways....
- Spiritual directors recognize their personal limitations ....

Chapter 5

Welcome and check-in [5 min]

- What would you like to share of your life as we gather?

Opening Prayer [2 min]

> *Lord, open us to your direction. Help us to listen with heart and soul when you speak.*
>
> *Open our hearts to the Holy Spirit who is our counselor, the giver of all good gifts, so we know where you are calling us at this moment.*
>
> *Open our eyes to the wonderful gifts you give us, so we can clarify what we cherish. Fill us with grace we need to release whatever binds us to sin, sorrow and shame.*
>
> *We especially ask for the grace to hear your voice during this meeting, so we can share our journey with openness and joy. Amen.*

Discussion [10 min]

- Intellectual and Professional Formation [See Appendix – Page 85].
- Guidelines for Ethical Conduct – Section II – Spiritual Director and the Directee.

- Read through and discuss the guidelines, below. Then answer the questions.

Questions for Reflection and Discussion on Ethics

- How might the guidelines help your practice of spiritual direction?
- Do you notice any ethical concerns in spiritual direction that these guidelines don't address?

Direction Session [10 min]

- Two directors model session.

Group Discussion [15 min]

- Group members discuss how the director used ethics mentioned in the talk.

Sharing on reflection questions [15 min/person]

- What am I discerning concerning the movement of spirits in me?
- How do I make decisions? How do I listen inside myself?
- As a result of being associated with this process, do I have any clearer indication of my call to the spiritual direction ministry?

Sharing Process:
1. Invite all to enter into the process.
2. Ask for silence to get centered and prepared to listen to the Spirit [1 min].
3. Individual shares [8 min].
4. Prayerful silence [1 min].
5. Group members respond to presenter (using

mirroring, clarifying, affirming, inviting to go deeper) [5 min].
6. Individual shares how he/she experienced the process [1 min].
7. Return to step 2 for the next person.

Book Discussion [15 min]

- Discuss chapters 5-8 Finding God in All Things.

Discuss Annotations of the Spiritual Exercises of St. Ignatius [20 min]

- Review and discuss Annotations 14, 15, 16.

Closing Prayer [02 min]

Thank you Lord, for teaching me about spiritual direction and the standards needed for the Spiritual Exercises of St. Ignatius.

You have given me a great gift – the ability to discern. And of course this gift requires work including prayer, introspection, and vulnerability. It also requires learning a new way of proceeding.

But I'm willing to commit to the effort. I want to serve you. So show me where you are calling me. Jesus, please open my heart to the information you impart, and to the beauty of your grace, given freely. You are so good, so generous, so loving. I proclaim your goodness and thank you for your generosity.

Help me to grow more humble, so I can become more human, more truthful, and more worthy of your love and grace. Let me be open to your will, no matter what that is.

Amen.

Evaluate the meeting [05 min]

- How was this meeting for you?

Homework

- Read chapters 9-11 in Finding God in All Things by William A. Barry, S.J.
- Meet with your spiritual director at least once.
- Pray every day, including the Examen.
- Attend any group meeting of the Spiritual Exercises.
- Read Annotations 17, 18, 22.

Spiritual Director's Formation

(From Appendix)

Intellectual Formation

From Guidelines for the Jesuits and their Colleagues in the Ministry of the Spiritual Exercises in the USA and English Speaking Canada.

Those who would give the *Exercises* to others will have:

- Received basic instruction on the structure and dynamics of the *Exercises*;
- Familiarity with the "text" of the *Exercises*;
- A basic understanding of the study of Sacred Scripture, especially of the New Testament;
- A basic understanding of Theology (especially Theology of the Trinity, of Christ, of Salvation, of morality, and of the Church).

Professional Formation

Those who would give the *Exercises* to others will have:
- received one-on-one mentoring[3] and supervision[4] by an experienced director through two retreats for those who give individually directed retreats;
- received mentoring by an experienced preacher for at least two retreats, for those who give conference retreats
- basic pastoral counseling skills, e.g. listening skills;
- training in preaching for those who give conference retreats.

Note: A person who does not have all the formal

training above but has been competently practicing in this field for some years can be recognized as having equivalent competence, knowledge and experience.

Standards for Spiritual Directors

Please read and discuss Appendix B, Section II.

II - Spiritual Directors with Directees

1) Spiritual directors initiate conversation and establish agreements with directees about …

2) Spiritual directors honor the dignity of the directee by …

3) Spiritual Directors maintain the confidentiality and the privacy of the directee by…

Chapter 6

Welcome and Check-In

- What would you like to share as we gather?

Opening Prayer

> *May it please the Supreme and Divine Goodness to give us all abundant grace ever to know his holy will and perfectly to fulfill it. ~ Amen.*

[This prayer was added to the end of many letters St. Ignatius wrote.]

Training [10 min]

- Finish discussing Appendix material.
- Read through and discuss *Guidelines for Ethical Conduct – Section III – Spiritual Director and Others*.

Question for Discussion

- How do you understand potential difficulties associated with "multiple roles and relationships," "imbalance of power," "boundaries" and "confidentiality?"

Observe a Spiritual Direction session and comment

Small Group Reflection

- Where am I in consolation and where in desolation in relationship to this process?

Sharing on reflection questions [15 min/person]

- What am I discerning about the movement of spirits in me?
- How do I make decisions about what to say?
- How well do I listen to others without feeling the need to talk about my issues?
- As a result of being associated with this retreat is there any clearer indication of my call to spiritual direction ministry?

Sharing Process:
1. Invite all to enter into the process.
2. Ask for silence to get centered and prepared to listen to the Spirit [1 min].
3. Individual shares [8 min].
4. Prayerful silence [1 min].
5. Group members respond to presenter (using mirroring, clarifying, affirming, inviting to go deeper) [5 min].
6. Individual shares how he/she experienced the process [1 min].
7. Return to step 2 for the next person.

Book Discussion [15 min]

- Bring discerners together (if separated) and discuss *Finding God in All Things* Chapters 9-11.

Spiritual Exercises of St. Ignatius Discussion [10 min]

- Review and discuss Annotations 17, 18, 22.

Closing Prayer

Show, Oh Lord, Thy ways to me and teach me Thy paths. Direct me in Thy truth, and teach me; for Thou art my God and my Savior.

~Blessed Peter Faber, S.J.

Evaluate Meeting [5 min]

Homework

- Read *The Art of Christian Listening* - Thomas Hart; Pages 1-60.
- Meet with your spiritual director at least once during the month.
- Pray every day, including the Examen.
- Attend Spiritual Exercises 19th Annotation group meeting (if available).
- Read Annotations 170-189 from the *Spiritual Exercises of St. Ignatius*.

Continuing Education/Formation

(Continued from Appendix A.)

Those who would give the *Exercises* to others will:

- Participate annually in a conference, formal course, workshop, or other structured program on spiritual ministry;
- Do regular reading in spirituality and religion;
- Maintain on-going supervision5 (one-on-one, group, peer, or with the retreat center director);
- Make a personal annual retreat;
- Continue to receive spiritual direction.

The Practice of Giving the Exercises

Those who give the *Exercises* to others will:
- Observe standard professional boundaries with regard to relationships, setting, place, content, etc.[6];
- Strictly observe confidentiality[7] (as limited by mandated reporting laws[8]);
- Consult and refer[9] when entering areas of unfamiliarity or non-competence (e.g., emotional or psychological disorder);
- Be faithful to the content of Ignatius's Spiritual Exercises, regularly reviewing the "annotations" and "rules"
- Evaluate each retreat carefully.

Guidelines for Ethical Conduct from Spiritual Directors International

Please read and discuss Section III.

III – The Spiritual Director and Others

1) *Colleagues* – Spiritual directors maintain collegial relationships with ministers and professionals …

2) *Faith Communities* – Spiritual directors maintain responsible relationships to communities of faith …

3) *Society* – Spiritual directors, when presenting themselves to the public, preserve the integrity of spiritual direction …

Chapter 7

Welcome and Check-In [10 min]

- What would you like to share briefly of your life as we gather?

Opening Prayer [2 min]

Lord, open our hearts to your Holy Spirit, our counselor, who gives all good gifts.

Open our eyes to the grace and help you provide, so we can clarify what we cherish and where you call us. Fill us with grace we need to release whatever binds us, or causes us to turn away from you. Make space in our hearts to reveal where you are calling us right now.

We especially ask for the grace to hear your voice during this meeting, so we can share our journey with openness and joy. Amen.

Review [3 min]

- Review Intern Schedule
- Review synthesis paper instructions

Book Discussion [30 min]

- Discuss what you've read in The Art of Christian Listening - Thomas Hart; Pages 1-60.

Sharing [15 min/person]

- Share where you are in your discernment process, in relationship to continuing into the Intern year.
    1. One person volunteers to begin speaking.
    2. Silence to center and prepare to listen to the spirit.
    3. Individual shares.
    4. Prayerful silence.
    5. Group members respond and mirror, clarify, affirm, invite to go deeper, challenge.
    6. Group members share thoughts on individual entering the Intern Program.
    7. Individual shares how this was for him/her
    8. Group takes a quiet minute to get ready to listen to next person.

Spiritual Exercises of St. Ignatius of Loyola [20 min]

- Review and discuss #170 - #189.

Observe a spiritual direction session and comment

Evaluate Meeting [5 min]

- How was this meeting for you?
- How was this year for you?
- How can we improve the process?

Closing Prayer [5 min]

- A Commendation to the Providence of God – Page 77. [From Hearts on Fire pg. 68.]

Homework

- Read The Art of Christian Listening - Thomas Hart; Pages 61- end.
- Continue to pray the Examen.
- See your spiritual director.
- Attend Spiritual Exercise 19th Annotation group meeting (if available).

Spiritual Director Intern Schedule

The following list will provide you with the expectations and duties of a good intern. Intern meetings consist of two parts: one hour of training and one hour of supervision. The Intern Program is provided at no cost to you.

Training

Each training presentation consists of four parts:
- Explanation and information on points from this part/movement of the retreat;
- How to facilitate this movement with your retreatant;
- Common blocks to this movement;
- Discussion and questions with other interns.

Supervision

As an intern, during the course of the nine-month training, you will:
- Present one supervision paper each month;
- Participate in ongoing review of strengths and growth; edges in spiritual direction ministry, including one-on-one meetings with a veteran director;
- Direct one to two people through the Exercises.

Month	Topic
September	Orientation, St. Ignatius' Life, initial contact with retreatant
October	Principle and Foundation
November	Loved Sinner / How to facilitate movement with retreatant
December	Call of the King and Introduction to Second Week
January	2 standards, 3 kinds of persons, 3 degrees of humility
February	Rules of Discernment
March	Passion
April	Resurrection
May	Learning to love like God, Evaluation

Intern Program Hours

Activity	Hours / Months	Total
Retreat Meetings	2.5 x 9 monthly meetings	22.5
Intern Program sessions	2 x 9 monthly meetings	18.0
Planning Meetings	2 hr. meetings x 9 months	18.0
Direction sessions (individual)	4x1-hour meeting/month x 9 months	36.0
Total Hours		94.5

Tentative Schedule for Group Meetings (Fill in dates)

September	December	March
October	January	April
November	February	May

Discerning Your Call

Written Assignment for Discerners

We are coming to the end of the Discernment Year, and so it is time make your decision. To do this, you will have the opportunity to practice discernment and write a paper on the subject for the rest of the group. Here's how to proceed.

Please pray with the following scripture before beginning your paper.

> *1 Corinthians 12: 4-11 "There are a variety of gifts, but always the same Spirit; there are all sorts of service to be done, but always the same Lord; working in all sorts of different ways in different people, it is the same God who is working in all of them...."*

Consider the sheet you've been given concerning the time you'll need to invest as an intern. Think about whether you have the ability to commit to that. If you feel called but don't have the time right now, you can choose to continue in the discernment program for another year.

Write a discernment paper describing your thoughts on becoming a director in the Spiritual Exercises (up to 3 pages). Focus mainly on whether you feel called or not to the intern program. State your reasons why, in light of the discerning you've done on your own and with this group.

Send copies of your paper to each person in this program two weeks before the final group meeting, including the facilitators, so we can discuss them at the final meeting.

Read all synthesis papers and write a recommendation about how you see each of the other discerners and their participation in the intern program.

The coordinator(s) will meet with each of you one-on-one following the final discernment meeting. He/she will let each of you know the decision for participation in the program.

Thoughts and Readings to Assist Your Discernment

Recognition of Gifts and Charism

Read 1 Corinthians 12: 4-11 – Variety of Gifts
1. What do I perceive as the special gifts of a spiritual director? What gifts have I seen in those who have directed me?
2. What gifts do I recognize in myself that might be offered in the service of others as a spiritual director?
3. Have others recognized or sought out my gifts in the area of spiritual companionship or direction?
4. Do I sense with myself a specific "charism" or gift for this work?

Concerns and Fears

Read Luke 9: 12-17 – Miracle of the Loaves and Fishes

What concerns or fears do I have about my ability to direct others? Where do I fear that I don't have enough of those who may come to me hungry?

What areas of need for personal growth am I most aware of at this time? How might they inhibit my ability to direct?

Am I faithful in my own spiritual growth through a habit of daily prayer, meeting with a spiritual director, and through openness to new learning?

Am I able to acknowledge my areas of poverty or lack of humility, to bring them before Jesus and trust that He can bless them and make them enough?

Ability to Commit Time and Energy

Read Matthew 13: 44-46 – Pearl of Great Price

In your imagination, weigh this 'pearl of great price' on one pan of a balance. On the other pan, consider:

The already-committed time or energy of my life to family, friends, joy, community

Time required for training and participation in the Exercises including:

- Director meetings
- Intern training and supervision
- Continuing education and classes
- Preparation time
- Saturday meetings
- Meet with retreatant
- My health, energy level, time required to pray and grow
- Finances

Closing Prayer - A Commendation to the Providence of God
~ St. Claude La Columbiere JS.

Loving and Tender providence of my God, into your hands I commend my spirit. To you I abandon my hopes and fears, my desires and repugnancies, my temporal and eternal prospects.

To you I commit the wants of my perishable body. To you I commit the more precious interests of my immortal soul, for whose lot I have nothing to fear as long as I do not leave your care.

Though my faults are many, my misery great, my spiritual poverty extreme, my hope in you surpasses all. It is superior to my weakness, greater than my difficulties, stronger than death.

Though temptations should assail me, I will hope in you; though I break my resolutions, I will look to you confidently for grace to keep them at last. Though you should ask me to die, even then I will trust in you.

For you are my Father, my God, the support of my salvation. You are my kind, compassionate, and indulgent parent, and I am your devoted child, who cast myself into your arms and beg your blessing, I put my trust in you, and so trusting, shall not be confounded.

Amen.

Chapter 8

Welcome and Check In [10 min]

- What would you like to share briefly of your life as we gather?

Opening Prayer [5 min]

- (Free Form) Ask the Holy Spirit to gift group members with openness.

Book Discussion [15 min]

- Discuss what you've read in *The Art of Christian Listening* - Thomas Hart; Pages 61-end.

Sharing [15 min/person]

Facilitator describes the structure of tonight's group process. Each discerner shares:
- Summary of his or her paper.
- I am, or I am not called to be part of the intern program, in light of the discerning done over the past year.

Sharing process: [15 min per person]
1. Invite the person to enter into the process.
2. Silence to prepare to listen with the Spirit.
3. Individual shares.
4. Prayerful silence.
5. Group members respond to presenter (mirror, clarify, affirm, invite, challenge a person to go deeper.)
6. Members comment regarding the individual entering the Intern Program.

7. Individual shares how this was for them
8. Group takes a short break, to prepare for next person.

Closing Prayer

- 1 Corinthians 12: 4-11 - Variety of gifts

Evaluate Meeting and Year

- How was this meeting for you?
- How do you evaluate the year?
- How might we improve the process?

Next Step - Individual meetings.

- Arrange a time and place for individual meetings between facilitator(s) and discerner.

Chapter 9

Individual Meeting Agenda

Greeting

Opening Prayer

- From the heart, or choose a scripture you like on discernment.

Discussion

- Commend the discerner for his or her efforts and commitment during the past year.
- Affirm the gifts you see.
- Review contents of his or her paper.
- Review comments made at the last meeting.
- Discuss growth edges, where he or she needs to grow, learn, or expand in order to continue.
- Confirm the discernment decision.
- Present a certificate of completion (if you prefer).
- Next Steps.

Closing Prayer

- From the heart – both share.

Appendix A

Guidelines for the Jesuits
And Their Colleagues
In the Ministry of the Spiritual Exercises

In the USA and English-Speaking Canada

From the Jesuit provincials of the United States and English Speaking Canada

We, the Jesuit provincials of the United States Assistancy, together with the Jesuit provincial of English Speaking Canada, recognize that the *Spiritual Exercises* of Saint Ignatius Loyola are a gift of the Holy Spirit to the whole Church. We realize that the Society of Jesus bears a special responsibility to preserve this gift and to promote its authentic use in its many applications and adaptations.[2]

Furthermore, we recognize that the spirituality and world view of the Spiritual Exercises inform all of the ministries and apostolic institutions of the Society. Therefore, we offer to Jesuits and our partners the following guidance for this ministry.

Care for and promotion of the *Spiritual Exercises* are collaborative efforts involving Jesuits and many others. The leadership, staffing, and governance of Jesuit-affiliated apostolic works, whether spirituality centers or educational institutions, are accomplished by lay persons, Jesuits, clergy, and religious working together.

---

[1] This document was formally adopted by the Jesuit Provincials of the United States and English Speaking Canada at their tri-annual meeting in October 12, 2009.

[2] This document distinguishes the terms "application" and "adaptation" according to the vocabulary of the *Spiritual Exercises*. "Application" refers to the act whereby an exercitant performs one or more of the specific exercises as intended in Ignatius' text. "Adaptation" refers to the practice of modifying one or more of the exercises or movements of the Exercises to fit the particular circumstances or capabilities of the exercitant. Annotation 18 defines and encourages "adaptation."

We expect that Jesuit formation will include an understanding of the structure and dynamics of the *Spiritual Exercises* and the preparation to give them in one or more modalities. In addition, efforts must be made to assist our partners in ministry with appropriate formation in the *Spiritual Exercises*.

We encourage Jesuit sponsored ministries to collaborate with other associations engaged in the ministry of the *Exercises*, especially the Jesuit inspired networks of lay persons who give the *Spiritual Exercises* in daily life. As far as possible, the Society of Jesus seeks to offer guidance, training, and support for these associations. The Jesuit Conference shall promote regular conferences and workshops on Ignatian spirituality in general and on the adaptation and the application of the *Spiritual Exercises* in particular.

Finally, we ask those Jesuits and Jesuit affiliated works whose ministry is giving the *Spiritual Exercises* to adopt the following guidelines. In keeping with the Principle and Foundation, use each guideline to the degree that it furthers the ministry.

This set of guidelines is currently in review as of July, 2015.

A. Guidelines for Those Who Give the Spiritual Exercises

Personal Spiritual Formation

Those who would give the *Exercises* to others will:
a. have completed the full four "weeks" of the *Spiritual Exercises* under annotation 19 or 20 (testified to by the director);
b. be in personal spiritual direction and making an annual retreat for at least two years;
c. have discerned a call to this ministry;
d. be a fully initiated Roman Catholic in good standing for at least three years or a similarly invested member of another Christian denomination who is respectful of, and comfortable with, Roman Catholicism.

Intellectual formation

Those who would give the Exercises to others will have
a. received basic instruction on the structure and dynamics of the *Exercises*;
b. familiarity with the "text" of the *Exercises*;
c. a basic understanding of the study of Sacred Scripture, especially of the New Testament;
d. a basic understanding of Theology (especially Theology of the Trinity, of Christ, of Salvation, of morality, and of the Church).

Professional Preparation

Those who would give the *Exercises* to others will

have:
- a. received one-on-one mentoring[3] and supervision[4] by an experienced director through two retreats for those who give individually directed retreats;
- b. received mentoring by an experienced preacher for at least two retreats, for those who give conference retreats;
- c. basic pastoral counseling skills, e.g. listening skills;
- d. training in preaching for those who give conference retreats.

Note: A person who does not have all the formal training above but has been competently practicing in this field for some years can be recognized as having equivalent competence, knowledge and experience.

---

[3] "Mentoring" is understood as the process whereby an experienced retreat director coaches, instructs, and guides a neophyte director.

[4] "Supervision" is here used in the sense in which the word is generally used in the helping professions. It refers to a practice whereby the retreat director reflects on and processes with another professional his/her own interior experience while giving a retreat

Continuing Education/Formation

Those who would give the *Exercises* to others will
a. participate annually in a conference, formal course, workshop, or other structured program on spiritual ministry;
b. do regular reading in spirituality and religion;
c. maintain on-going supervision[5] (one-on-one, group, peer, or with the retreat center director);
d. make a personal annual retreat;
e. continue to receive spiritual direction.

Those who give the *Exercises* to others will:
a. observe standard professional boundaries with regard to relationships, setting, place, content, etc.;[6]
b. strictly observe confidentiality[7] (as limited by mandated reporting laws[8]);

---

[5] see footnote 3 above.
[6] The Jesuit Conference recommends the Spiritual Directors International Guidelines for Ethical Conduct.
[7] Nothing learned from the directee, including the directee's name, may be disclosed to another without the directee's permission. The director must inform the directee that he or she (the director) is being supervised and will make every effort to protect the directee's identity.
[8] These mandated reporting laws vary by state.

The Practice of Giving the Exercises

    c. consult and refer[9] when entering areas of unfamiliarity or non-competence (e.g., emotional or psychological disorder);

    d. be faithful to the content of Ignatius's *Spiritual Exercises*, regularly reviewing the "annotations" and "rules";

    e. evaluate each retreat carefully.

---

[9] When dealing with psychological or emotional issues that impair a directee's judgment (e.g., trauma or addiction), the director may, with permission, consult a professional or may recommend that the directee see a clinician or specialist.

B. Guidelines for Jesuit Retreat Houses and Spirituality Centers

Mission: The Jesuit Retreat House or Spirituality Center

    a. has a formal vision/mission statement;
    b. concentrates its programs on the *Spiritual Exercises*, their application and adaptation;
    c. reviews and applies directives from the General Congregations (including ecumenical and interfaith dialogue);
    d. reviews and applies province and assistancy apostolic priorities;
    e. employs a process of review and application for new program development with appropriate evaluation;
    f. has programs that reflect the mission of the house/center, responds to the needs of the local and universal Church, and seeks to meet the needs of various generations and cultures;
    g. has approved safe environment programs for ministry, especially to minors and vulnerable adults, according to the province and diocesan policies.

Liturgical Life:

The liturgies celebrated in the house or center:
    a. Reflect good contemporary Church practice consistent with local diocesan norms;
    b. support and enhance the programs of the house/center;

c. model good sacramental liturgy (Eucharist, Anointing, & Reconciliation);
  d. foster a prayerful environment for the programs in the house or center.

Practice

Of Ignatian Conference Retreats:
  a. renews and deepens the retreatants' life of faith and practice of religion;
  b. is an application of Annotation 18 and should include both an effort to dispose the retreatants to graces of Ignatius's *Spiritual Exercises* and instruction in living the Christian faith;
  c. is carefully adapted to the group, with respect to stage of life, gender, socio- economic status, ethnicity, culture, etc.
  d. encourages retreatants for further grow in their spirituality (e.g. 19th annotation, weeks of director prayer, etc.).

Viability

The Jesuit Retreat House or Spirituality Center:
  a. attracts a population of retreatants that reflects the Church in the region and supports continuing growth;
  b. engages in strategic planning;
  c. works toward adequate financial resources and systems of accountability to maintain the facility and to support the mission;
  d. has competent and responsible financial management;

e. conducts fund-raising for program and capital needs;
f. successfully advertises and promotes the sponsored programs;
g. has buildings and grounds that are appropriate to the mission;
h. is welcoming;
i. is safe and well maintained, clean and attractive
j. renovated and improved to support the evolving mission.

Leadership

The leadership of the Jesuit Retreat House or Spirituality Center:
a. is structured to meet the mission and particular needs of the institution;
b. includes an effective board that exercises, in partnership with the province, responsibility for the ministry
c. animates staff, volunteers, and retreatants in analysis, problem solving, and planning for the future effectiveness of the ministry.

Staff

The pastoral/ministerial staff of Jesuit Retreat Houses and Spirituality Centers:
a. has qualifications consistent with *Guiding Guidelines*, Part A.
b. is guided by policies that are clear and provided to all the staff (i.e., provided in a staff handbook that includes policies on professional conduct, hiring, terminations, etc.)
c. receives just compensation;
d. receives support for continuing formation/education;

Evaluations

a. The institution uses evaluation instruments completed by attendees[10] and visiting directors, reviews the data, and makes changes based on the data.
b. The staff annually reviews its ministry and implements changes based on self- evaluation and client-evaluation.
c. The director of the institution assures the evaluation of staff.
d. The board and/or province representative assures the evaluation of the director.
e. The province engages in annual evaluation of the institution and its ministry.

Administration:

Those in leadership in Jesuit-sponsored ministries will:
a. have received training in administration and management;
b. have received initial and ongoing formation in Jesuit spirituality and mission;
c. observe professional guidelines;
d. work collegially with boards, staff, and provincial representatives; and
e. receive ongoing professional development.

---

[10] For 19th and 20th Annotation Retreats, the director will be evaluated by his or her directee.

Appendix B - Guidelines for Ethical Conduct

Ethical conduct flows from lived reverence for life, including self, and others. This reverence extends into the spiritual direction relationship. These guidelines are meant to instruct as well as inspire spiritual directors in the SEEL program to pursue integrity, responsibility, and faithfulness in their ministry and service of others.

Based on the Guidelines for Ethical Conduct
Spiritual Directors International, 2014

I. The Spiritual Director and the Self

Personal Spirituality

1. Spiritual directors assume responsibility for their own personal growth. They:
    a. Participate in regular spiritual direction.
    b. Follow personal and communal spiritual practices and disciplines.
    c. Participate in church events and celebrations.

Formation

2. Spiritual directors engage in ongoing formation and continuing education. They:
    a. Continue to discern their call to the ministry of spiritual direction,
    b. Nurture in self-knowledge and freedom,
    c. Cultivate insight into the influences of culture, social-historical context, environment, and institutions,
    Study sacred scripture, theology, spirituality, psychology, and other disciplines related to spiritual direction.

Supervision and consultation

3. Spiritual directors:
    a. Engage in regular supervision from peers or a mentor,
    b. Seek consultation when necessary from and/or with other appropriately qualified persons.

Personal Responsibility

4. Spiritual directors meet their needs outside the spiritual direction relationship in a variety of ways. They:
    a. Balance time for spiritual practices, work, leisure, family, and personal relationships to promote self-care,

    b. Recognize and address the difficulties that multiple roles or relationships might pose to the effectiveness or clarity of the spiritual direction relationship,
    c. Remove oneself from any situation that compromises the integrity of the spiritual direction relationship.

Limitations
5. Spiritual directors recognize the limits of:
    a. Energy - restrict the number of spiritual directees
    b. Attentiveness – schedule appropriate space between meetings and directees to be effective,
    c. Competence - refer directees when necessary to other appropriately qualified persons.

II. The Spiritual Director and the Spiritual Directee

Covenant

1. Spiritual directors initiate conversation and establish understanding with spiritual directees about:
   a. The nature of spiritual direction,
   b. The roles and responsibilities of the spiritual director and the spiritual directee,
   c. The length and frequency of spiritual direction sessions,
   d. Compensation, if any, to be given to the spiritual director or institution,
   e. The process for evaluating and terminating the relationship.

Dignity

2. Spiritual directors honor the dignity of the spiritual directee in many ways:
   a. Respect the spiritual directee's values, culture, conscience and spirituality
   b. Inquire into the motives, experiences, or relationships of the spiritual directee only as necessary,
   c. Recognize the imbalance of power in the spiritual direction relationship and take care not to exploit it,
   d. Establish and maintain appropriate physical and psychological boundaries with the spiritual directee,
   e. Refrain from sexualized behavior, including, but not limited to, manipulative, abusive, or coercive words or actions toward a spiritual directee.

Confidentiality

3. Spiritual directors maintain the confidentiality and the privacy of the spiritual directee. They:
   a. Protect the identity of the spiritual directee,

b. Keep confidential all oral, electronic, and written matters arising in the spiritual direction sessions,
c. Recognize and disclose to the spiritual directee the limitations of confidentiality of electronic communications,
d. Conduct spiritual direction sessions in appropriate settings,
e. Address legal regulations requiring disclosure to proper authorities, including but not limited to, child abuse, elder abuse, and physical harm to self and others.
f. Use pseudonyms for a directee whenever he or she is used in supervision.

III. The Spiritual Director and Others

Colleagues
1. Spiritual directors maintain collegial relationships. They:
    a. Develop intra- and interdisciplinary relationships,
    b. Request that any spiritual directee who is in therapy inform the therapist about being in spiritual direction,
    c. Secure written releases and permission from spiritual directees when specific information needs to be shared,
    d. Respect any directed ministers, clergy, spiritual care providers, and other professionals by not disparaging them or their work.

Faith and Spiritual Communities
2. Spiritual directors maintain responsible relationships. They:
    a. Remain open to processes of corporate discernment, accountability, and support,
    b. Draw on the teachings and spiritual practices of the spiritual community appropriately.
    c. Respect the spiritual directee's relationships to his or her own communities.

Society
3. Spiritual directors, when presenting themselves to the public, preserve the integrity of spiritual direction by being in right relation with persons and organizations. They:
    a. represent qualifications and affiliations accurately,
    b. define the particular nature and purpose of spiritual direction,
    c. seek opportunities to be spiritually available to the underserved,

    d. live in an ecologically responsible and sustainable manner,
    e. respect all persons.

For Further Discussion:

How do we as a community understand potential difficulties associated with "multiple roles and relationships," "imbalance of power," "boundaries," and "confidentiality"

Terms

Spiritual directors – trained men and women who have discerned a call from God and the community to accompany people through the Spiritual Exercises in Everyday Life (19th Annotation of Spiritual Exercises of St. Ignatius).

Formation – The SEEL community is formed through a three-year process. 1) Person successfully completes the Spiritual Exercises in Everyday Life. 2) The community believes they are ready, they are invited to a year of discernment, reading, and studying the Spiritual Exercises of St. Ignatius. 3) An internship year of study, monthly supervision, and directing another through the Spiritual Exercises.

Supervision – A group process that evaluates a specific direction session using the form from Supervision Handbook. It requires a written paper as well as evaluation of a specific direction session.

Spiritual Exercises in Everyday Life (SEEL)

SEEL directors have been called by God and the community to accompany others in their search for God. We respond to this call, tending the holy, by way of the Spiritual Exercises of St. Ignatius, 19th Annotation.

Purpose and History

SEEL is a group of lay people trained in spiritual direction for, and dedicated to, providing the Spiritual Exercises of St. Ignatius, 19th Annotation.

This spiritual community serves and supports the ministry in the context of the Catholic Church. It is affiliated with Jesuits West US Province. SEEL strengthens the faith of our community by accompanying and teaching those who are seeking spiritual guidance.

SEEL Tri-Cities began in 1985 in Richland WA. In the ensuing years, the community has expanded to provide the Spiritual Exercises of St. Ignatius to the greater Mid-Columbia region. SEEL Tri-Cities is a 501(c)(3) not-for-profit organization incorporated in the state of Washington, USA.

Made in the USA
Columbia, SC
07 December 2018